The Bright Side
of the Dark

The Bright Side of the Dark

Mayuresh Kulkarni

RESOURCE *Publications* · Eugene, Oregon

THE BRIGHT SIDE OF THE DARK

Resource Publications
An Imprint of Wipf and Stock Publishers
199 W. 8th Ave., Suite 3
Eugene, OR 97401

www.wipfandstock.com

PAPERBACK ISBN: 978-1-6667-5617-3
HARDCOVER ISBN: 978-1-6667-5618-0
EBOOK ISBN: 978-1-6667-5619-7

09/13/22

CONTENTS

Lyrical flights
directly go to God
thematical one,
linger at the gate
for the query of God!

Grace

REALLY

They say that
they relate to my pain,
but what about that
immortal and unfaithful spark
which has ignited the flame
and which has burnt alive
those innocent dews
on the roses?
I am talking about
the bottom of the ocean
and you are thinking about
the height of the sky!
You may write my destiny
on the sands of the desert,
but rains will not spare you
The blood has already turned blue,
how long the veins
are supposed to
carry the burden?
Thousands of years
after I disappear,
you may find a fossil
deep in the forest
which will have the
faint impression of my pain
and then don't dare to claim,
that you still relate
to my pain!

THE CONFESSIONS OF CHRIST

Let me commit those
divine sins and
I am not afraid of
your penalties!
But first wash
your hands in the
pool of blood of those
whom you murdered
and colour your eyebrows
with the sperms of the
horses you ride
You may chase me
But beware of the foxes
running with me
They will throttle the
cords of your neck
The iceberg has started melting
like a golden pillar
I can clearly see my sins
floating on it
But still you can't fix me
The well I jumped into,
is full of a magical darkness
without the slightest of the
reflection of the blue sky
Still I travel through
till the bottom of the earth
only to realise that,

it is the earth
who is revolving
around the moon!
Now tell me,
who has deceived whom?
They will now
pray for life
but the brutality
will not listen to
their last screams
Midnight will innocently
blame the full moon
They will pretend
to keep the silence
But illusions don't
live long!
The Constitution of the nation
Is being drafted impartially,
denying the justice to those
who fought for it
I can see the candles
burning in my blood
Now the heaven
is not too far
I am sitting on the
edge of the wall,
looking at the universe
in the golden twilight
My sins are inherited
by the birds
of my fraternity
flying deep
into the sky,
to let my soul
peacefully die . . . !

TO ALL MY YOUNG FRIENDS OVER THERE

I am living
in my shell
though you have
locked me in the
prison cell
The guards are
marching around me
but I don't care!
You can detain my body
but you can't detain
my thoughts!
Soon, the regime will collapse
and the guards will
fall in love with me
Prison will be broken
to release my bones
The impatient mothers
will hold their wombs
in peace for a while!
Now, I will lead the flag
in the new era
I want that rebellious
youth to march with me,
who have the springs
of enthusiasm oozing
from the fountain
of their hearts

and the capacity to paint
their dreams on the sky
I will inject my blood
Into them
Let the poison spread
with the speed
of the vicious snake
Let the minds be blown
with the winds of the storm
The horizons are looking
at you with a
profound hope!
Be ready to execute
the heads with your swords
It's a dawn of a
New civilization
Let us burn this
impotent system
But don't worry,
the ash will write
a new script for you!
Let us bless this world
with the eternal values
to be cherished forever
Let us free this mankind
from the hatred, lust, religion
and from the chronic
disease of corruption
Love has no limits
to engulf another planet
Let the tulips kiss
the soul of the stars!
Have the nerves of steel,
the courage of a lion,

the brains of the mathematician
and the passion of the eagle
to fly to the summit!
Believe me, my young friends,
you can certainly do it
You are the mentors of the
new civilization ... !

THE ETERNAL MOMENTS

Last evening
I took my piano
to the graveyard
to entertain the ghosts
No No, those eternal souls
didn't complain
because they were busy
fighting with each other
for the scarcity of the
space in the coffins!
I played some disturbing
symphonies of Mozart
on the special requests
of the ghosts
which they had listened to
abruptly at the time
of their death
I was really moved
to see the tears
in their eyes while
hanging to the
branches of the tree,
but suddenly one
eternal soul came to me
and whispered in my ears
"Don't be fool,
they are pretending!"

When I turned to him,
I was thrilled to find
that those eternal souls
were envious of the ghosts!
One ghost came to me
swimming through the air
He had humor in his eyes
when he said,
"Don't take him seriously,
he was a missionary!"
I looked up
at the stars
they were smiling at me
"Well done boy,
these poor ghosts hardly
afford such a divine music!"
I spent some time
with the ghosts
Some told me their
unfortunate stories of
how they were murdered
mercilessly by the Boyfriends
of their unfaithful wives
I really couldn't understand
how to react!
However, I enquired with them
that why they have gathered
in such a large number
The old ghost answered,
"Boy, today is our carnival
Today is the lunar eclipse!"
They offered me the wine
made of the blood of
the finest grapes

All of a sudden one
eternal soul came
shouting at the ghosts,
"Get out, get out immediately!
Your time is over!!"
The old ghost smiled at me
"Don't worry, he was a
Watchman of this graveyard
who died last summer
of cancer!"
Soon I left the place
leaving my piano
for them
I really had a great time
with those lovely ghosts
and a bitter experience
with those horrifying
Eternal souls!

THE BARS OF THE CAGE

Those blessed, gifted and fortunate ones
whose fortunes are seduced with
their charm of the present
and their past is
as elegant as the
crafted diamond!
While in my case,
my fate has seldom
smiled at me
My fortunes are scared with
the glimpses of my present
which has inherited
the shadow of my past
as dark as the
midnight skies!
Stars in my fate
have gathered like the
Conspirators of Julius Caesar!
Cassius definitely has a wicked smile
as he finally has my most
Noble friend Brutus
in his side!
The storm has begun to roar
The cross silver lightnings
are indicating the
signs of the evil
but I am unmoved,

because I had the
intuition of the traitors
What they don't understand
is that I have that mighty
element to rise above all
like the forces of the nature
I am the Lion in the cage
who will one day
break open those bars
with the wisdom of God,
with the skill
of the magician,
with the power of the
hundred elephants
and with the pen
in my hand!
They might have written me off
but I am here to
write their last Will!
I know that the
eggs of the serpent
have to be crushed
before they are hatched
as they inherit the
same poisonous thoughts!
I don't care about my
so called dreadful fate
I will write my own destiny
and then their faces will look
as gloomy, pale and shameful
as the defeatist of war
having no courage
to give me a straight look!
I don't mind even if

they steal my sword,
I can still fight
with the shield!
Let them assassinate me
as brutally and as fiercely
as they can
with their daggers
and let my best friend Brutus
strike me that
last heavy blow
at the footsteps of
the statue of Pompey
still I won't say,
"You too, Brutus???"
because I know that
it is none of his fault!

A HOLY MERCHANT

If you purchase my sins
I will donate you the
buds of my wisdom!
But don't be flattered,
you yourself will
have to put the
nails to your coffin
The graffiti on the wall
is now clear,
that unfortunate child
has to die
but the history repeats
again and again,
it is not the end of
the mankind
You may fix the
triangle in a circle
but still I can carve
a hole in the center
I may take a rebirth
but not in the
wounds of the tears,
but in the pours
of the earth
from which the
blood is leaking
drop by drop
but you have

no right to
defame him
who has crafted
this universe with
the meticulous ease
If you sow my sins
in the bed of
the ocean
then thousands of years later
the volcano will erupt
from the heart
of the mountains
which will melt
the snow on the
last planet from the earth!
Gods have gathered
in the sky
Let the oil in the
intestine of the earth
start burning
You will see a
violet flame on the
forehead of the sky
The ship has sunk
with the captain
on the deck
Gods have started
retreating from the battlefield
but still you have got
the best deal
in the market,
my wisdom will stand
the test of time
until you return
to the holy nest!

THE ORIGIN OF THE OCEAN

You may study minutely
the groves on the
skin of my brain
but you won't find
the proof
You may pump
the liquid detectors
in my heart
but you won't
find the evidence,
you are looking for!
You may puncture
my lungs
only to find that
it does not have
oxygen
Finally, you turn to
the spine
and to your utter surprise
you find in the place
of the spinal cord,
a thin spiral of the
glowing pearls!
You are now wondering
what kind of species
the poet is?
Finally, in sheer frustration

you are about to
execute my head
to search for the gland
which secretes that
insane poetic pain!
However, all of a sudden
my body starts shivering and
changing its colour
from blue to green
and slowly an Angel
immerges from my blood
with the magical batten
in his hand!
"Stop your futile search at once
Your science will
never understand
the system of the poet
The origin of the pain
you are looking for,
is not within his body
but the seeds of it
lie in the
sacred crimes
committed by him
in his last birth unconsciously,
which he inherits
not by the genes
but by his unfortunate fate!
Even your great Einstein
who coined the Theory of Relativity
but had he been the
Professor of literature,
still he would have coined
the same theory,

describing the poetic energy
as the mass of the pains
suffered by the poet
multiplied by the
speed of the imagination
with which he is gifted!
You may give him
a benefit of doubt
or let that thought
be pregnant with
the suspicion
that the poet is the
most privileged child
of God!
Good by friends!"
The Angel disappears!
They stitch my body
with the disgusting looks
only to be buried
next to Christ!

THE ODD MAN THERE

They said,
you are Psychologically challenged
I said, may be
but I love to take
the challenges!
I know i am not
like you
I don't get ecstatic
in joy and the
miseries don't
take me down
I make my own rules
though I live in
your hypocrite world!
My sins can penetrate
the ovaries of
your moral values
because your values
are corrupt from
the ancient times!
I see beyond and
I can read between the lines
I don't care for you
and am not here
to pamper your
false egos
I carry the burns of fire

with the grace
of the ice
I know, you certainly
don't like that
you always pray
to God that
I should cry
at least once
but you envy me
because it is the God
who cries for me!
I can't relate to
your so called
legal system
and your way
to punish the offenders
but don't forget,
it is the same
legal system
which has punished
Jesus,
but he knew that
you can nail his body
but not the soul!
So you have no moral
or the ethical right
to celebrate his birthday
on the day of Christmas
because it is your forefathers
who had taken him
away from us
and snatched that
Blissful light from us
to lead the mankind

for a journey of
a dark tunnel
where the war has overpowered
the seat of love
and the hatred has
fallen in love with
the human relations!
Now please don't cry,
it is nothing but the
Crocodile tears
and the height of hypocrisy!
Though you dress up
in the warmest of the clothes,
your hearts and minds
are as naked as
the animals!
Ruthless times has
witnessed the world wars
and awaiting for
many more to follow
I know am not like you,
obviously not!
You are those poisonous
germs on the softest
bud of the Lotus,
but don't worry
you won't succeed
in getting inside
as long as I am alive!
I have the guts
to stand against you
not because I
worked on them
but because I am

born with it
I may die after
a few years
but my vigor and passion
will be carried in the
next generations to come
by my fellowmen
to whom you will
again outcast as the
Psychologically challenged!

WHO KILLED THE BUTTERFLY

Once upon a time,
the butterfly was
waiving its wings
on the tip of a
yellow rose
with the smile
on its lips and
dreams in the eyes
It's wings were
crafted with the
rare design
of reddish blue
colours of the dawn
The freedom was
it's race, unaware
of the restrictions as if,
the sovereignty and discretion
were the
colours of its wings
It really had a good
taste of life to choose
the best flower to
bed in the valley
Oh no! What's this?
The snake bites!
Vision started disappearing
The lungs were struggling

to breathe the air
The heart started
missing the beats
Clouds started making
the sky nervous
Will they burst?
The earth is scared of
hugging the pains again!
The darkness starts
roaming the space
The life takes the turn
Contexts change
The fate drags it
mercilessly into
the endless tunnel!
Dirty water replaces
the blood in the body
They compel to wear
a distorted personality
Struggle is inevitable
Heart is pumping
the wounds all over
The mental disorders
started ruling the brain
Senses slowly died
like a leprosy
Insults, intimidations,
provocations were
singing the song
from the bottom
of their hearts
The rotten eggs was
now the taste of life
Miserable was the

State of affairs
Shattered were the dreams!
When tried to look back
even could not realise
what was the price paid
Frustration poured through
the layers of the skin
Finally, pains crossed
the superlative degree
Blood appeared in the eye
and not the tears!
But tell me, who killed
the butterfly?

HOLD YOUR BREATH

Let me write a script
with the tip
of the mountain
with the ink of the
boiling red Lava
flowing from it
on the surface
of the blue ocean
which can be easily
read by the
stars in the sky
for the infinite years
on the background of
the delicate symphony
played by the gentle wind
on the piano of the forest
ignoring the existence
of the negligible mankind
to mark the beginning
of that glorious ceremony
to crown the queen of
the earth on the
throne of the universe
which moment is
graced by Gods
gathered in the sky,
showering the reddish

flowers of the delicate
rays of the evening sun
and the soft
blue petals of the
drops of the rain
to gift the Queen
with the precious necklace
of that sparkling rainbow!

GOSPEL

"I too,
walked up
that treacherous path
of Villa Dolorosa
till its
fourteenth Station,
off course
without carrying the
burden of that
heavy Cross,
but still,
I collapsed finally,
for carrying physically
the weight of history
and . . . .
. . . .
a guilty mind!!!

THE AWARDS

They did not choreograph
my life
and they never will be,
because i could never pay
for their
professional fees
Nevertheless,
they were generous enough
to do the honors
by putting those
chronic twists
to my
barely hanging
rope
which loyally accompanied me
for the rest of my
life!
But now,
no more sufferings
as I have already left
the shores of life
We see the Sun and
the Moon
and get fascinated about
their marvels,
but do we ever think of
hundreds of

such suns and the moons
glowing brightly
in the sky
millions of galaxies
away from us?
Who are we
to evaluate anybody
who could not
able to deliver
in their life times,
but who knows
hundreds of years after
they perish,
they will be admired
and applauded
for their work
which was
left to be acknowledged
by us
Some gallantry awards
are given posthumously
to those brave men
who did not survive
to see the final day
of victory
Who knows
what is stored in the
embryo of time?,
One day
the Noble Prizes too
will have to be given
posthumously
to those men
and women

whose greatness
those panel judges
failed to appreciate
in time
At that time
it is the award
that will be honored
and not
their winners!
It's not written in the
destiny of some
to see the light
at the end of the
tunnel,
but it anyway
doesn't make
their struggle and
the journey
less valuable
Therefore,
history should never
under estimate
the future!
Well,
let's not be so eager
to predict
from the obvious,
at least
try to go
beyond the
borders!!

STAY ALIVE

Am feeling something strange
at this hour;
what is that can you figure out?
Is it a sadness or dejection
of the circumstances
or despondency or dispirited?
but why?
Is it because
somebody has kicked the bucket
or has been seriously ignored?
Please don't open
the Pandora's box
am not ready to
weep again
not be doleful or glum,
but tell me are you
Interested in the
physical beauty
or the matured mind?
Hey man,
just throw that awesome
burden of sorrows
and taste the slice of
cheerful atmosphere
Are you embarking on
that vibrant journey?
yes I am

it resonates my soul
to explore and embrace
a new land
where nobody has
gone before!
But is it the joy of
Vasco de Gama
successfully paving the
new path
or the misery of
Columbus
of landing on a
wrong destination?
To me both are equally
ecstatic and throbbing
my heart beats!
No more melancholy.
Indulge in the nostalgic reminiscence
Is it an anecdote or
a fairy tale?
Yes now I see a
beautiful red Poppy
in a barley field!!

ZEAL

They said,

"Man is the captain of his destiny!"

I agreed to it without any inhibitions,
but when i started steering my ship
in the clear blue waters,
all of a sudden
the sea became rough
and soon,
the worst of the storm
engulfed my ship!
I tried hard
to get out of it
in a right direction,
however
the magnetic needle
of the compass
started behaving
like an insane child,
i looked at the sky,
but the sky was looking
as black as of that
dreadful night.
Finally, I jumped into the
waters.
But friends,

this is not the
end of the story!
i decided not to give up,
and as i landed
on the sea bed,
i started collecting the oysters
throughout the night,
relentlessly!
At last,
a few moments to dawn,
I found the one
I was looking for.
I gently opened the shell
and a precious
sublime white glowing pearl
was smiling at me!!
You see,
I might not be
the captain of my destiny,
but i think,
life is not all about
mastering the controls,
but it is,
to survive through
until you find
the right oyster!!!

PYRAMID

Through the storms
of the sands in the
heated desert,
you see a huge
triangular structure
of stones with
no door and windows
Thousands of years ago,
they brought me here,
taken out the blood, flesh,
bones and the heart
out of my body
They thought I am dead
confirmed it again and again
before leaving me
here forever
Since then am locked here
cut off from the world
living in a vacuum
Off course, the sketches on
the walls do accompany me!
Shakespeare once wrote about
'The comedy of errors'
but here it was certainly
'The tragedy of errors!'
Sometimes at night,
the stars in the sky

do try to penetrate
this structure,
but in vain!
I can only feel their
shadows moving inside
Storms, thunders, rains, cold
are immune to me
The peace inside is
so dangerous that
at times the sound
of my pulse also
becomes irritating!
But I have seen the
fall and the epitome
of the mankind
I have seen the
human race evolved
from generations to generations
I have seen values diminishing
and the religions emerging
I have experienced that
immortal truth in the heart
of Gautam Buddha when
he was enlightened
under that divine tree
of 'Bodhivruksha' at Gaya
I have felt the pains
of the virgin Mary
when she was about
to deliver Christ
I have seen the battles
won and lost
I have seen the
lust of power

murdering their dear ones
I have seen the
seductive beauties
in their most cunning roles
I have seen the
kingdoms created
and the regimes vanished
I know the exact length
and the diameter of the
tip of the nails
pierced in the
body of Christ
But I have also seen
the joy of wisdom
concurring the devil
The satisfaction of the
sacrifice over the victory
The love wining the hatred
I have seen it all!
But am not
alone here
her fond memories
are always with me
through thick and thin
I have always felt her
warm touch and her
breaths have refreshed
my gloomy atmosphere
like a pleasant perfume!
I have always
felt her presence
when her shadow
passed over me
Her long hairs have

almost suffocated me
and I still remember the
taste of her lips
when we last met!
Am sure, I would not
have been able to
live inside for ages
without her
My soul is heavy
with her tears
May be one day,
she will free me
from here!

THE SHADOW OF A SHADOW

The beauty of my nation
certainly lies in its countryside!
Those lush green fields
waiving their bodies
on the tune of
a windy day
Those colourful wild flowers
smiling at you
from the edges of the fields
Those blue mountains
standing as firm and solid
like the armed soldiers
sporting the graceful
white caps of the clouds
The sky has spread infinite
with that vibrant blue
instigating me to fly!
And the mother of the countryside
she is flowing
protecting its border
with a deep patience
and calmness
ready to wash
all your sins
to make your soul pure!
She is as transparent
as her heart,
the crystals of the sands

sleeping on her bed
are shining in the sunlight
Her bank is paved with
the hard black rocks
inviting me to take
a nap on them
The birds are eagerly
flying to their nests
and the cows and buffaloes
are swinging their bells
tied around their neck
in a joy of returning to home
That small reddish farmhouse
is a cherry on that green canvas!
Sun has set
The sky is turbulent
A very delicate slice
of the moon has
slowly immerged from
the mountains
Am trying to look
in her eyes
but her shy looks
are preventing me
Her innocence is adding
an aroma to the
whole atmosphere
She is looking as beautiful
as the Princess of a fairy tale!
The mischievous breeze
is playing with her hairs
There is certainly a
romance in the air!
I gently hold her hand
and she looks at me

Her eyes are saying
everything to me
which is inscribed
in her heart
No words are spoken
No commitments are made
No music is played
in the background
The silence is giving a sanctity
to those immortal moments!
I think 'love' is a very
thin word to describe
the intensity of those emotions!
We may not relive
those moments again
but that earth, that sky,
that moon and the stars,
those mountains
and that river
are all witness to
our tender ties!
Whenever I remember
those moments,
my eyelids try their best
to cover-up the trauma
but those tears
are not just the
layers of the wound
but are the symptoms
of my deceased soul
which I can never interpret
in any language!
May God give me
the courage to
withstand such moments!

www.ingramcontent.com/pod-product-compliance
Lightning Source LLC
Chambersburg PA
CBHW071744020426
42331CB00008B/2170